Occupational Safety and Health Act of 1970

"To assure safe and healthful working conditions for working men and women; by authorizing enforcement of the standards developed under the Act; by assisting and encouraging the States in their efforts to assure safe and healthful working conditions; by providing for research, information, education, and training in the field of occupational safety and health."

This publication provides a general overview of a particular standards-related topic. This publication does not alter or determine compliance responsibilities which are set forth in OSHA standards, and the *Occupational Safety and Health Act of 1970*. Moreover, because interpretations and enforcement policy may change over time, for additional guidance on OSHA compliance requirements, the reader should consult current administrative interpretations and decisions by the Occupational Safety and Health Review Commission and the courts.

This information will be made available to sensory impaired individuals upon request. Voice phone: (202) 693-1999; teletypewriter (TTY) number: 1-877-889-5627.

Safe Work Practices for Shipbreaking

Occupational Safety and Health Administration
U.S. Department of Labor

OSHA 3375-03
2010

Cover photo courtesy of H. Reid, Metro Machine Incorporated.

Start to Finish

This guidance document is not a standard or regulation, and it creates no new legal obligations. It contains recommendations as well as descriptions of mandatory safety and health standards. The recommendations are advisory in nature, informational in content, and are intended to assist employers in providing a safe and healthful workplace. The *Occupational Safety and Health Act* requires employers to comply with safety and health standards and regulations promulgated by OSHA or by a state with an OSHA-approved state plan. In addition, the Act's General Duty Clause, Section 5(a)(1), requires employers to provide their employees with a workplace free from recognized hazards likely to cause death or serious physical harm.

Contents

Introduction

Shipbreaking is a unique part of the maritime industry, primarily involving the dismantling and disposal of obsolete U.S. Navy and Maritime Administration ships, as well as commercial barges and mobile offshore drilling units. For many years, much of this work was contracted to overseas companies. However, in recent years the exporting of ships from the United States to foreign countries for scrapping has come under criticism due to concerns over worker safety and health, and adverse environmental impacts. As a result, the exporting of ships for scrapping was stopped by the Navy in December 1997 and by the Maritime Administration (MARAD) in January 1998.[1] Consequently, shipbreaking by domestic companies is rapidly growing, and there is a need to improve shipbreaking (e.g., dismantling, ship recycling, or scrapping) processes to ensure the safety and health of these workers.

Dismantling of vessels is usually conducted at a pier, drydock, or dismantling slip and includes a wide range of activities, from removing all gear and equipment to cutting down and recycling the ship's structure. The structural complexity of ships makes shipbreaking a challenging process. It involves many safety, health and environmental issues, including exposure to asbestos, toxic fumes, hazardous materials, noise, falling objects, lead and electrical shock, as well as dangers associated with heat stress, falls, heavy materials handling and fires.[2] In light of the need to improve and manage the hazards associated with shipbreaking, this document is to be used as a basic guide for employers involved in shipbreaking activities. The hyperlinks to OSHA, international, and other documentation provided throughout this publication give more detailed information and recommendations.

This document does not cover all of the regulations governing the occupational safety and health aspects of shipbreaking. However, it highlights important information through references and hyperlinks to OSHA regulations that can be used to help employers develop a comprehensive Safety and Health Management System (SHMS), encompassing all aspects of a facility's shipbreaking procedures and processes. The appropriate Code of Federal Regulations (CFR) provisions must be incorporated in all safety and health plans, and the safety processes and programs must be managed to reduce risk and provide a safe and healthful worksite for all workers. In addition, employers must be aware of and comply with all local and state regulations, which may be more stringent than federal requirements.

Interagency Work Group

In December 1996, the Department of the Navy, the Defense Logistics Agency (DLA), the U.S. Maritime Administration (MARAD), and the U.S. Coast Guard (USCG), along with other involved agencies, began meeting quarterly to discuss shipbreaking program improvements and to share evaluation procedures and oversight information. In February 1998, the group was formally chartered as the Interagency Panel on Ship Scrapping. The work of the group resulted in a set of recommendations that were presented in the April 20, 1998, *Report of the Interagency Panel on Ship Scrapping*. The recommendations covered many aspects of the shipbreaking industry, including contracting improvements, performance bonds, data gathering and pilot projects, polychlorinated biphenyls (PCBs) guidance, regulatory oversight and international issues.

Under the category of regulatory oversight, the panel recommended that the Environmental Protection Agency (EPA) and OSHA, in conjunction with DLA, the U.S. Navy, and MARAD, develop a comprehensive compliance guide. This guide, entitled *A Guide for Ship Scrappers*,[3] outlines the relevant environmental and occupational safety and health requirements applicable to shipbreaking. The guide contains recommendations for completing shipbreaking operations in a safe and environmentally compliant manner.

Steps in Shipbreaking Process

After removal from the fleet site, the vessel is towed or self-propelled to the site where scrapping will occur. The vessel is then scrapped while being moored to a pier, anchored, beached, or dry-docked (including graving docks). Most scrapping is performed pier-side in slips, which are typically dredged openings that are adjacent to a shipping channel. Slips are approximately 400 to 1,000 feet long and 100 to 140 feet wide at the entrance. Shipbreaking is generally performed by cutting away large sections, which are then moved to shore for further dismantling. A large winch at the head of the slip is used to drag the hull farther out of the water as work progresses. Throughout the scrapping process, it is important for the appropriate safety precautions to be determined and followed to effectively protect personnel. The scrapping process[4] usually occurs in a series of steps:

- **Conduct a vessel survey.**[5] Diagrams of all compartments, tanks and storage areas are used (or prepared, if not available) to identify areas that may contain hazardous materials such as fuels, oils, asbestos, PCBs, lead and other hazardous wastes. Sampling is conducted using a systematic approach, usually starting in the compartment that will be cut first. In many cases, a facility will presume that certain items contain hazardous materials and dispose of them as such, in lieu of sampling. In such cases, the employer must use proper engineering controls and work practices to ensure that workers, involved with and in the vicinity of the removal, are properly protected from exposure (e.g., through the use of wet methods, or wetting agents, and vacuums with HEPA filters).

- **Remove fuels, oils, other liquids and combustible materials.** The removal of fuels, oils and other liquids (e.g., bilge and ballast water) from the ship generally occurs throughout the shipbreaking process. Bilge water is sampled and disposed of appropriately. In addition, during the vessel scrapping process, water may accumulate due to rain, firefighting activity, or use of hot work cooling water, and will have to be properly removed. The U.S. Coast Guard requires booms to be placed around the vessel to help contain any spills (See OSHA publication 3172 (2001), *Training Marine Oil Spill Response Workers Under OSHA's Hazardous Waste Operations and Emergency Response Standard*). Following removal activities, a marine chemist[6] certifies that the vessel is safe for entry and safe for hot work. A competent person must continually monitor these areas to ensure that they are still in compliance with the marine chemist's certificate.

- **Remove equipment.** Fixtures, anchors, chains and small equipment are removed first. Large reusable components (e.g., engine parts) are removed as they become accessible. Propellers also may have to be removed so that the hull can be pulled into shallow water.

- **Remove and dispose of asbestos and PCBs.** Both asbestos-containing materials (ACMs) and PCBs are usually removed in two stages. Prior to cutting away a section of the vessel, ACM is removed from areas that are to be cut and PCBs are removed from areas that are readily accessible. After the vessel section has been moved to

shore, the remaining ACMs and PCBs are removed as they become accessible during the dismantling of the vessel section. The engine rooms usually contain the most asbestos and, therefore, take the longest for asbestos removal to be conducted.

- **Prepare surfaces for cutting.** Following the removal of combustible materials, asbestos and PCBs, paint or preservative coatings must be stripped from surfaces to be cut (29 CFR 1915.53). Hard-to-remove materials on surfaces may require specific cut-line preparation, such as grit blasting or flame removal of paint,[7] which can expose workers to toxic metals and volatile components of paint. Appropriate precautions must be taken (e.g., the use of airline respirators) to effectively protect personnel performing the removal, as well as those workers in the immediate area (see 29 CFR 1910.134).

- **Cut metal.** During the cutting phase, the upper decks, superstructure and systems are cut first, followed by the main deck and lower decks. Metal cutting is usually done manually using oxygen-fuel cutting torches, but may be done with shears or saws for nonferrous metals. Typically, as large parts of the vessel are cut away, they are lifted by crane to the ground where they are then cut into specific shapes and sizes required by the foundry or smelter to which the scrap is shipped. As cutting continues and the weight of the structure is reduced, the remaining hull floats higher, exposing lower regions of the hull. Ultimately, the remaining portion of the hull is pulled ashore and cut.

- **Recycle or dispose of materials.** Scrap metals, including steel, aluminum, copper, copper nickel alloy and lesser amounts of other metals are sorted by grade and composition, and sold to remelting firms or to scrap metal-brokers. Valuable metals such as copper in electric cable that are mixed with nonmetal materials may be recovered using shredders and separators. The shredders produce a gravel-like mixture of recyclable metal particles and nonmetal "fluff," which is not recyclable and needs to be sampled for hazardous materials and disposed of according to state and federal regulations. The metals are then separated from the fluff using magnetic separators, air flotation separator columns, or shaker tables.

Initial Visit to Vessel to Determine Suitability for Scrapping

Before any work is conducted, an initial visit to the vessel is required to determine its condition. During this visit, the following must be identified: the hazardous materials (e.g., lead, asbestos, PCBs) that must be removed from the ship, the hazards that workers could be exposed to during the scrapping operations, and the condition of the ship, including its suitability for towing and seaworthiness. From the information obtained, a sampling plan[8] must be developed to address environmental remediation and the health hazards[9] identified, including the special tools and equipment that will be required to ensure worker safety. When workers are aboard the ship for this assessment, those who are required to work alone must be checked on frequently, as required by 29 CFR 1915.94. To comply with this requirement, employers should make arrangements with the ship's custodian for worker escorts during this visit. The custodian should be consulted with to identify unknown hazards such as missing decking, open holes, or areas that may need to be gas-free.

Navy vessel pier-side for shipbreaking, Ex-USS Forrestal.

Occupational Safety and Health Administration

The Hazard Communication standard, 29 CFR 1915.1200, requires that employers communicate information about health hazards to workers and that they have material safety data sheets (MSDSs) available for all hazardous materials handled or used in the shipbreaking process. OSHA standards for specific substances are generally performance based and require the protection of personnel from hazards through compliance with permissible exposure limits, exposure monitoring, medical surveillance, use of respirators and protective clothing, and other requirements (see 29 CFR 1915, subpart Z). Some specific hazards of shipbreaking include:

- Freon[10] commonly found in refrigeration systems that, if released, could evaporate rapidly to create atmospheres immediately dangerous to life or health (IDLH).

- Halon[11] and carbon dioxide[12] in fire suppression systems that can create IDLH atmospheres if they are released into spaces. Manual and free-flood automatic fire-suppression systems must be physically isolated or employ other positive means to prevent discharge before any hot work is permitted in spaces protected by such systems (29 CFR 1915.506).

- Hydrogen sulfide[13], a colorless, toxic and flammable gas that can result from the decomposition of microscopic marine life killed by Aqueous Film Forming Foam (AFFF) mixed with seawater in AFFF wet firefighting systems.

- Carbon monoxide (CO)[14], a colorless and odorless gas that is produced by the combustion process such as welding, spontaneous combustion, and internal combustion engines. Prolonged exposure may result in headaches, nausea, dizziness and ataxia.

- Metals of concern may include:
  - Lead[15] in paints and some greases, or possibly as tetraethyl lead[16] for use as an additive in fuels;
  - Mercury[17] in gauges, tank-level indicators, or fluorescent light tubes;
  - Tributyltin oxide[18] on underwater hull plates;
  - Chromates[19] in paints and varnishes;
  - Cadmium in electrical and electronic equipment; and
  - Arsenic paints.

- Oxygen deficiency[20] due to rusting in tanks that have been sealed for long periods of time.

- Toxic contamination due to hazardous cargoes that may have been carried in tanks.

- Asbestos exposure for workers removing asbestos-containing thermal insulation; handling circuit breakers, cables, and cable penetrations; and removing floor tiles (from asbestos in the mastic and in tile). Additional concerns can arise from handling and removing gaskets from piping systems and from electrical systems. Asbestos may also be found in some molded plastic parts. All asbestos must be identified, removed and handled in accordance with 29 CFR 1915.1001. Asbestos removal is also regulated by the EPA under the asbestos National Emissions Standards for Hazardous Air Pollutants (NESHAP), 40 CFR 61 Subpart M. Many states require, and OSHA recommends, that an AHERA-qualified (Asbestos Hazard Emergency Response Act of 1986) asbestos inspector identify all asbestos-containing materials prior to beginning ship-breaking oerations. Some states also require that employers notify their environmental regulatory agencies prior to conducting asbestos removal operations.

- Polychlorinated biphenyls (PCBs) in rubber products such as hoses, plastic foam insulation, cables, silver paint, habitability paint, felt under septum plates, plates on top of the hull bottom, and primary paint on hull steel.

Additional information on health hazards associated with shipbreaking can be found in the OSHA Shipbreaking Fact Sheet.[21]

Photo: Al Miller

The Roger Stahl towing the Saginaw from Duluth on 10/24/99.

Towing the Vessel

Dead-vessel tows are regulated by the U.S. Coast Guard at 33 CFR 165 et seq. Administrative procedures for towing vessels are established by local Coast Guard Sectors, so employers should contact their respective Captain of the Port (COTP) to determine local policy; see Port Directory. Usually, a request for a dead-ship tow is required to be submitted at least 48 hours in advance, if the tow is within the port, and seven days in advance, if the tow is outside the port. Typically, this task is handled by the contracted towing company.

Generally, the request must contain the following information about the towed vessel: name, call sign, flag, length, draft, sail height, and the type, amount, and locations of oil and other hazardous materials

onboard. However, the required information may vary depending on the port. Tank diagrams are recommended to detail the location of oil and other hazardous materials. The request must also contain the total number of tugs and their horsepower, place of departure and destination, the date and time of departure, the duration of the tow, and the name and 24-hour telephone number of the responsible party. Indicate if an unusual tow configuration will be used or if the request is for more than one towed vessel.

Depending on the particulars of the vessel being towed (e.g., age, extended lay-up status, vessel condition, etc.), the COTP may require that additional safety precautions be established before the tow is authorized. This may include requirements such as obtaining a marine surveyor's report, verifying the vessel's seaworthiness, or allowing a representative from the Coast Guard to examine the vessel to verify seaworthiness, pollution potential, and the adequacy of the towing arrangement. Such a report will include the recommended towing configuration, a condition inspection to evaluate seaworthiness, a determination of which personnel will be allowed on board during the tow, and any other special instructions to allow for a safe tow.

In certain circumstances an International Load Line Exemption Certificate or a Coastwise Single Voyage Load Line Certificate may be required in accordance with 46 CFR 42 Subchapter E (Load Lines). To make this determination and schedule an examination, requests for tows offshore (e.g., beyond the boundary line) must be submitted seven days in advance.

Mooring the Vessel

Vessels that are intended for pier-side scrapping need to be properly secured using approved mooring lines and a mooring plan reviewed by a qualified professional, such as a naval architect or marine engineer. The facility should have a Heavy Weather Plan, which includes additional mooring requirements for high and low tides, hurricanes, and other adverse weather conditions. Mooring bits should be engineered to have sufficient strength to withstand forces imparted by all weather conditions. It is recommended that ships not be moved during winds exceeding 25 knots.

Personnel assigned to assist in line handling should be experienced in line handling and must wear personal flotation devices[22] (PFDs) when there is a potential for falling into the water, as required by 29 CFR 1915.152(a). Personnel must be kept clear of the lines and never stand in the bight of a line. Nylon lines, primarily used on older ships, are subject to atmospheric damage (e.g., sunlight, weathering, etc.) and may break without warning, releasing large amounts of energy capable of killing or maiming workers.

Spill-containment booms must be placed around all vessels, and personnel should be trained in the procedures for opening and closing the booms. Care should be taken to keep small boats, located between booms, from being crushed due to unanticipated vessel movement. Fenders or other breasting devices should be used to prevent such an incident. Operators of small boats must wear U.S. Coast Guard-approved PFDs and have on board a life ring with 90 feet of line.

Workers must be denied access to the vessel until a gangway, ladder, or ramp meeting the requirements of 29 CFR 1915.74(a) and (b) and 29 CFR 1915.75(a) thru (d) is provided. Particular attention should be paid to the trim of the gangway, ladder, or ramp, where the fall or rise of tides may cause the angle to become unsafe, or pull away from its support. Means should be provided to deny access to the vessel by unauthorized personnel during non-work hours.

Vessel in dry dock for scrapping.

If work is conducted at night, adequate lighting[23] must be provided and maintained at all times as required by 29 CFR 1915.92(a). In shipbreaking operations, the ship's lighting may be difficult to maintain and, therefore, should be considered unreliable. If ship's lighting is used, a secondary means of lighting (e.g., temporary lighting or personal flashlights) must be provided as required by 29 CFR 1915.92(e). Personal flashlights must be intrinsically safe or explosion-proof as required by 29 CFR 1915.13(b)(9). Light-emitting diode (LED) flashlights are recom-

mended for use in gas-free spaces due to their small size, durability and dependability.

Example of temporary lighting.

Hauling the Vessel

It is important, before hauling a vessel[24] out of the water, that an evaluation of the stability of the vessel be conducted. Forces can develop that could make the vessel unstable and cause it to tip over. Personnel must not be aboard a vessel while it is being pulled ashore, since it is possible for the vessel to topple over or for sections to break, creating severe hazards for workers onboard. A naval architect or marine engineer who has extensive experience docking ships should evaluate the ship for stability prior to hauling the vessel to ensure a safe operation.

Hauling machines and chains or wire ropes are used in the hauling process to move vessels in the water and on shore. This equipment is affected by the weight of the vessel, the incline of the slope, the friction between the hull and the slope, and any change in the rate at which the vessel is hauled. When more than one chain or wire rope is used, the loading must be equalized among the chains or wire ropes to ensure that no single leg is overstressed. It is imperative that the equipment operators are aware of the hazards associated with the hauling process and have the ability to quickly compensate for torque or variation in pitch.

Hauling machines usually consist of a train of gears, operated by electric motors turning one or more toothed chain wheels driving the hauling chain. The moving parts of hauling equipment must be guarded as required by 29 CFR 1915.115(b).

Steel hauling chains with appropriate pitch and uniform link dimensions should be used for hauling the ship. Because of their high tensile strength and the ease with which they can be connected with special hauling shackles, which are as strong as or stronger than the chain itself, most scrappers find chains more durable and economical than the best wire rope. The ability to measure the strength of chains is a major advantage that chains have over wire ropes. These chains, fitted over alloy steel wheels, have a small pitch diameter that permits hauling heavy loads with relatively small hauling machines. A chain swivel is recommended to prevent excessive twist, which could cause an overload of one section of chain.

It is particularly important to protect chains from abrasion caused by sliding through sand, gravel, or silt. In some installations, a means for washing the sand off the incoming chain should be provided. Chains should be inspected frequently for wear and removed from service when they become excessively worn or do not meet the manufacturer's recommendations. Caliper measurements can be used to determine the strength and corresponding safe live load of chains at any stage of wear.

Rivers are often subject to wide ranges of water level, with periods of low water lasting several months, interchanged with shorter periods of high water. The vessels traveling such rivers are, of necessity, shallow-draft, flat-bottomed craft of light construction. A side-hauling method may be used when dealing with such vessels in rivers, but would not be appropriate for hauling ocean-going vessels. This method should be chosen only after careful study by a qualified naval architect or marine engineer to determine if it is a suitable method.

The principal technical disadvantage of the usual side-haul arrangement, handled by several parts of chain or wire rope, is that the load on any component cannot be accurately determined. Therefore, it is impossible to use an equalizing system. Consequently, it is necessary to use oversized chains or wire ropes to avoid possible overload.

Some employers use all-terrain forklifts or bulldozers to pull vessels ashore. When this practice is used, it should be done only in accordance with the manufacturer's recommendations. This system should be evaluated and approved by a naval architect or marine engineer before being used. No modifications or additions may be made to a forklift to allow hauling of vessels without the manufacturer's prior written approval as required by 29 CFR 1910.178(a)(4). Any equipment used for this purpose should be protected with a rollover protective structure, and operators should wear seat belts. Additionally, workers should be kept clear of the line of pull of the chains or wire rope used, and a suitable guard may need to be installed to protect the operator of

the hauling machine from being struck by a breaking chain or wire rope.

Planning

It is important for employers to have a safety and health management system (SHMS) in place that encompasses all aspects of the facility's shipbreaking procedures and processes. The SHMS should consist of a technical plan, safety and health plan, and an environmental technical plan, which can be altered for each specific job. A **written technical plan** should outline the scrapping process, schedule, cut lines, and other engineering factors specific to each project, to ensure that the vessel is scrapped in a systematic manner to protect property and personnel. Drawings of the vessel should be obtained and broken down by work areas to allow a naval architect or marine engineer to develop a cut plan so that the weight and stability of each vessel section can be assessed at each stage to ensure a safe operation. A **safety and health plan** or **manual** should cover all aspects of the shipbreaking process and specify actions to be taken in the event that an emergency occurs. An **environmental technical plan** should address remediation of all hazardous materials. Each plan must be developed in accordance with federal, state and local laws. Daily production meetings should take place to discuss the day's events, upcoming critical processes and procedures, and any safety considerations or special instructions needed to complete the day's tasks safely. A morning **safety talk** should be scheduled to discuss safety and health issues that will be faced on that day, or other topics for educational and special emphasis purposes.

Breaking the Vessel

One of the first steps in breaking the vessel is the removal of hazardous and flammable materials, which is often called the drilling and draining phase (or pumping phase). Drilling refers to the act of drilling holes in systems to allow the release and capture of fluids in the systems. It may also involve opening drain ports already installed in the system. Holes are drilled at the lowest possible points in the system to ensure that the system is completely drained of fluids. Draining involves removing all hazardous fluids and materials from the ship's systems including hydraulic, cooling, high-pressure air, steam condensate, preservatives in rudders and skegs, and fire-suppressant materials such as AFFF (aqueous film-forming foam), halon and carbon dioxide. It is important to consider the hazards that this process creates, and they should be treated accordingly. Personal protective equipment (PPE) must be provided to personnel to prevent them from coming into contact with liquids, oils, greases and materials that could cause skin and eye irritation (29 CFR 1915.152(a)). All PPE should be selected by appropriately trained personnel and examined for proper fit. Further, atmospheric testing by a competent person is required while these systems are being drained (29 CFR 1915.12(a)). Testing must be performed in each space or area that workers are required to enter or conduct work. This testing must occur in the following sequence: oxygen content, flammability and toxicity.

No hot work is allowed in spaces that contain active fixed fire-extinguishing systems that have not been isolated to prevent discharge. If this precautionary step is not followed, the system could release its contents into the space, producing a dangerous atmosphere.

As hazardous materials are drained from systems, the materials should be segregated by substance and kept separate. Mixing hazardous materials may cause uncontrolled chemical reactions between materials, resulting in exothermic reactions (excessive heat or fire), release of toxic gases, or other reactions that could injure personnel or cause an environmental spill.

Several procedures/processes may occur simultaneously during the drilling and draining phase, including hazardous materials remediation, removing recyclable items, and extracting easily removed interior components. This process helps remove as many components as possible from the interior of the vessel, creating a tunnel effect, to allow cutting to begin from the top down. Cutting then proceeds from each end of the vessel, working towards the center of the vessel (see the diagram below – Module Cut Plan).

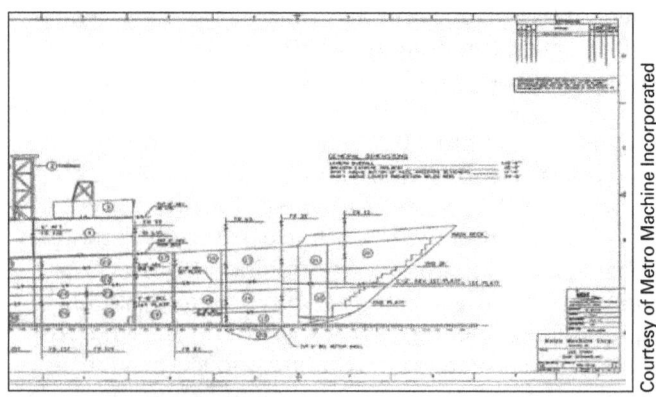

A sample Module Cut Plan.

Courtesy of Metro Machine Incorporated

This multifaceted approach requires excellent planning and constant safety oversight so that workers are aware of what operations are ongoing and where they are occurring aboard the vessel. The daily safety talk can be a valuable tool for informing workers of planned operations for the day.

As the work progresses, good housekeeping must be maintained to reduce hazards and provide safe work surfaces and areas for workers. Solid wastes should be promptly removed and properly disposed of to aid in maintaining a safe work area.

Photo by Chris Tyree, *The Virginian Pilot*

Worker torch-cutting scrap metal from vessel.

Burning Equipment

Burning equipment used in cutting metals must be provided with regulators and flashback arrestors should be installed. Lighter-than-air gases (e.g., acetylene, natural gas) are recommended because they do not pool in low areas as heavier-than-air gases (e.g., argon, propane, carbon dioxide) tend to do. Lines should be inspected frequently for damage and should be routed to avoid damage and to avoid tripping hazards for workers. Lines must not be left in enclosed spaces while unattended for longer than 15 minutes (29 CFR 1915.503(b)(2)(ii)). Pressure-drop tests or other positive measures should be conducted on the lines each time that they are connected to a manifold to ensure their integrity, so that there are no leaks within the burning system (29 CFR 1915.503(b)(2)(iv)). At the end of each shift the torch lines should be rolled back to the manifold. Fittings for gas lines must be incompatible with respiratory equipment to avoid mixing toxic gases with breathing air.

Compressed-gas cylinders must not be taken into confined spaces. During storage, oxygen cylinders must be separated from fuel-gas cylinders by a minimum of 20 feet or by a 5-foot high barrier with a minimum half-hour fire resistance rating. When cylinders are not in use, they must be disconnected and have valve protection caps in place. Cylinders should be stored in an upright and secured position away from high traffic areas.

Cold Cutting

Cold cutting of vessels presents numerous hazards to workers. Therefore, it is imperative that reciprocating saw blades are kept sharp to prevent malfunctions that can lead to possible injuries. This practice will speed production as well. Since saws create noise sufficient to cause hearing loss, hearing protection must be provided to and be used by workers operating or working in close proximity to the saws (see 29 CFR 1910.95). Additionally, ergonomically-designed gloves should be used to minimize vibration exposure to workers. The employer must ensure that the power supply to reciprocating saws is provided with ground-fault circuit interrupters (see 29 CFR 1910 Subpart S). Electrical cords must be maintained in sound condition and routed or protected so as to prevent damage to the cords and avoid creating a tripping hazard for workers.

Mobile Hydraulic Shear Cutters

Mobile shear cutting is prevalent in shipbreaking and presents several hazards to personnel. Workers must not place any part of their bodies in the danger zone of the equipment (e.g., the shear area). When this type of machine is mounted as an attachment on a backhoe or excavator-type machinery, the swing radius should be barricaded to prevent workers from coming into the pinch-point area between the rotating structure of the machine and its drive carriage or other fixed objects, such as the part of the ship being scrapped. Care should be taken to cut materials to prevent recoil and to keep large pieces from striking or falling on workers.

Mobile hydraulic shear cutters used in shipbreaking.

Occupational Safety and Health Administration

Shoreside Processing of Metals

Scrap metals, including steel, aluminum, copper, copper nickel alloy, and lesser amounts of other metals, are sorted by grade and composition and sold to remelting firms or to scrap metal brokers. Valuable metals, such as copper in electric cable, that are mixed with nonmetal material may be recovered using shredders and separators. The shredders produce a gravel-like mixture of recyclable metal particles and non-metal "fluff" that is not recyclable and needs to be sampled for hazardous materials and disposed of according to state and federal regulations. The metals are then separated from the fluff using magnetic separators, air-flotation separator columns, or shaker tables. Machine guarding must be provided in accordance with 29 CFR 1910.212 and 29 CFR 1910.219. Guards should be interlocked to shut down the equipment in the event that the guard is opened. Noise exposure must be controlled in accordance with 29 CFR 1910.95. An industrial hygiene assessment of metals exposure must be conducted and controls implemented to maintain worker exposures within acceptable limits. Asbestos must be removed in accordance with 29 CFR 1915.1001 before processing scrap metal. Measures must be taken to prevent skin contact with polychlorinated biphenyls (PCBs). Additionally, PCBs must be cleaned from cut lines of materials that are to be cut by burning (see 29 CFR 1915.53(d)(1)).

Care must be taken to ensure that workers do not position themselves beside or below a section being cut, where falling pieces of scrap or the section might strike them. Pieces being cut often become unstable, shift, fall or slide. Therefore, workers must be positioned so that they are not subject to being struck by shifting materials (see 29 CFR 1915.116(j) and (k)). Several fatalities have been recorded where scrap metal pieces or sections crushed workers walking through cutting areas.

Fall Protection

Falls are a major hazard in shipbreaking due to the ever-changing work environment. Continuous cutting of the vessel weakens the structures or sections and creates new openings and deck edges, making fall protection a necessity. Workers need to wear safety harnesses and be tied off when near open holes and deck edges. Anchorage points for each positioning device system must be capable of supporting at least double the potential impact load of a worker's fall (29 CFR 1915.160(a)(3)). In addition, lifelines must be kept clear from sharp edges to avoid the lines from being cut or damaged (see 29 CFR 1915.159(c)(4)). Although the requirement in 29 CFR 1915.73 ("Guarding of deck openings and edges") does not apply to shipbreaking, it is recommended that barriers be placed around or near deck edges and openings whenever feasible.

Examples of fall protection.

All photos courtesy of Metro Machine Incorporated

Side shell cuts are made, leaving 42-inch high bulkhead at the deck level for fall protection.

The lack of a requirement to guard deck edges and openings does not remove the employer's responsibility to protect workers from fall hazards through the use of appropriate fall protection systems. In certain circumstances, during the shipbreaking process, workers are required to work from aerial lifts and man lifts that are suspended by cranes to reach elevated areas for cutting. In these situations, it is also important for appropriate fall protection to be used.

Fire Prevention and Protection

Subpart P - Fire Protection in Shipyard Employment, 29 CFR 1915, requires employers to have an overall fire suppression program that establishes the location, type and capacity of firefighting equipment such as extinguishers, fire hoses and standpipes, smoke detectors, automatic sprinklers and other fixed firefighting systems in accordance with applicable fire codes. Employers must have a written plan in place that provides for the routine inspection, maintenance and replacement of this equipment and must require training for new workers and refresher training for all shipyard workers. The written plan must include procedures for the control of fire hazards, such as flammable and non-flammable compressed gases, ignition sources, combustible materials, welding and hotwork operations and must include procedures for evacuation. The employer's evacuation plan must include the following: emergency escape procedures; procedures to be followed by workers who may remain longer in the worksite to perform critical shipyard operations before they evacuate; procedures to account for all workers after an emergency evacuation is completed; preferred means for reporting fires and other emergencies; and the names or job titles of the workers or departments who may be contacted for further information or explanation of duties.

The hazards associated with the use of fixed fire-extinguishing systems on vessels and vessel sections have long been recognized by the U.S. Coast Guard as evidenced by Coast Guard Commandant Notices and Instructions that date from 1978. The International Maritime Organization (the United Nations' specialized agency responsible for improving maritime safety and preventing pollution from ships) has also addressed these hazards by issuing regulations that are part of the International Convention for the Safety of Life at Sea. 29 CFR 1915.506(b) requires employers to protect their workers who may be exposed to a dangerous atmosphere caused by a fixed fire-extinguishing system by either physically isolating the system, disconnecting or blanking, or using other positive means to prevent the system's discharge. In shipbreaking operations, OSHA recommends that the system be physically disabled. In general, there should be no work conducted with the system activated. However, should such a situation occur, the employer must ensure that workers are trained to recognize the system's discharge and evacuation alarms, appropriate evacuation routes and hazards associated with components of the system.

Employers must have a written fire watch policy that specifies the necessary training of workers, their duties and personal protective equipment (PPE) to be used. This policy may be part of the overall fire safety plan or separate, but must be effective in protecting workers from injury. A firewatch must be posted while hot work is being performed when any of the following conditions are present: slag, weld splatter, or sparks; unprotected combustible materials or insulation; and heat radiation or conduction on insulated pipes, bulkheads, decks, overheads and partitions (see 29 CFR 1915.504). It is important that workers assigned to firewatch duty are not tasked with any additional duties while hot work is in progress. In addition, the firewatch must be able to communicate with the workers performing the hot work, as well as any personnel that may be affected.

Method used for emergency response and fire-prevention planning.

Emergency Response

In addition to compliance with 29 CFR 1915.502, which includes a fire safety plan, OSHA requires compliance with 29 CFR 1910.38 and 29 CFR 1910.39 for emergency response and fire prevention planning. Employers do not need to have separate emergency response plans as long as the plan covers the applicable general industry worker emergency plan and fire prevention plan provisions, as well as the shipyard employment fire safety plan. A mustering plan for each jobsite should be incorporated in the emergency response plan to account for all workers in the event of an emergency where evacuation is required. Each plan or combination of emergency response plans must be in writing, kept in the workplace and be available to workers for review.

Drills

A fire response organization, as defined in 29 CFR 1915.509, may include (1) fire brigades, (2) shipyard fire departments, (3) private or contractual fire departments, or (4) municipal fire departments.

While larger shipyards may have their own fire responders, smaller shipyards often use an outside source, typically the local fire department. These municipal or other fire departments may have little experience in fighting fires in shipyards, especially on vessels. Fighting vessel fires can be more complicated than traditional firefighting because outside firefighters seldom have the opportunity to learn the layout of the vessels. Additionally, vessels being scrapped have constantly changing structures. Therefore, proper coordination, familiarization, training and drills are necessary to ensure the safety of outside firefighters who respond to shipyard fires. See 29 CFR 1915.505 for OSHA safety requirements.

If an outside fire response organization is used, OSHA requires employers to communicate with that organization about facility layout and familiarization, and coordination protocols (29 CFR 1915.505). OSHA believes that any fire response organization that expects to respond to shipyard fires will benefit from this coordination. They will be able to respond to fires quickly and effectively, thus enhancing safety for the shipyard workers and their own fire response team members.

In coordinating drills and other communications with an outside fire department, employers must discuss the types of fire suppression incidents to which the fire response organization is expected to respond to and procedures for obtaining help from other fire response organizations. Additionally, methods of familiarizing the external fire response organization with the layout of the facility or worksite, including access routes to controlled areas and site-specific operations, occupancies, vessels or vessel sections and hazards should be discussed. The employer must ensure the standardization of all fire-hose couplings and connection threads throughout the shipyard and on vessels or vessel sections by providing the same type of hose coupling and connection threads for hoses of the same or similar diameter. See 29 CFR 1915.505 (f)(2)(ii).

Responders to shipyard fires encounter a complex set of hazards involving buildings, as well as vessels in drydocks, wet slips, or pier-side. Fire responders need to be prepared to safely and successfully handle a wide range of fires from flammable liquids in a storage room of a shipyard building, to oil-soaked rags in the engine room of a ship. The fires could include: combustible materials (such as wood, paper, or cloth); flammable or combustible liquids (such as oil, fuels, paints, or chemicals); insulation and other materials that may give off toxic gases and smoke during a fire; electrical components (such as energized motors, circuit controls, transformers, or wiring); or even combustible metals (such as magnesium or titanium).

Rescue

A rescue team must be established to respond promptly to rescues required in confined and enclosed spaces or other areas where dangerous atmospheres may be present. The rescue team can be composed of workers, or it can be an outside team that meets all the applicable requirements of 29 CFR 1915.12(e)(1). When an outside rescue team is used, they should be given a tour of the employer's facility to ensure familiarity with the operations and to identify any special concerns for rescue. They must be given an opportunity to conduct drills on board a vessel being scrapped in accordance with 29 CFR 1915.12(e)(1)(iii).

Lifesaving Materials

At least one ladder[25] meeting the requirements of 29 CFR 1915.158(b)(5) must be available near each floating vessel on which scrapping work is being conducted. Depending upon vessel length, one or more liferings[26] meeting the requirements of 29 CFR 1915.158(b)(1) thru (4) must also be provided. Although they are not required for shipbreaking operations, OSHA recommends that at least one lifesaving skiff be immediately available at locations where workers are working over or adjacent to water.

Hazardous Material Spills

Spill kits should be provided that contain an adequate quantity of suitable materials for spill containment and cleanup. The contents of these kits should be restored after each use to ensure that adequate materials are available to allow workers to respond safely to future spills. All applicable environmental regulations should be consulted to ensure that response and reporting requirements are met. Only fully qualified and properly equipped personnel are allowed to respond to hazardous material spills.[27]

Energy Control

Every effort should be made to take all mechanical and electrical systems to a zero energy state during the drill and drain phase of breaking the vessel. However, to provide adequate lighting for workers, the ship's lighting system[28] is often maintained. It may also be desirable to maintain the electrical distribution system, which can be more dependable, rather than using shore-based temporary services to provide power to electrical equipment and tools. When this is done, the employer must ensure that the integrity of electrical systems is maintained in a safe manner, including guarding of live parts and grounding by implementing electrical energy control procedures in accordance with 29 CFR 1910 Subpart S to ensure the safety of workers.

Mechanical systems should be isolated from their energy source and rendered inoperative, drained and depressurized prior to working on them. Each isolation device, controlling the energy to a mechanical system, should be physically located and disabled. In addition, workers must not be allowed to work in or on a lifeboat until the boat is secured in accord with 29 CFR 1915.96(a). Cradles or carriages on marine railways in a hauled position must be secured in accord with 29 CFR 1915.115(e)(1).

Before hot work is permitted in areas where free-flooding, automatically activated fire-suppression systems are installed, the system must be physically isolated or other positive means used to prevent an accidental discharge. For additional information on the hazards of fixed extinguishing systems, see 29 CFR 1915.506.

Medical

The employer must provide a first-aid room in close proximity to workers or a first-aid kit for each vessel on which work is being performed. In either case, a qualified person must be close at hand to render first aid to workers. Employers must take the necessary precautions to protect persons administering first aid, as well as nearby workers who may come into contact with blood and other potentially infectious materials (see 29 CFR 1910.1030 and OSHA Bloodborne Pathogens Fact Sheets). When work is being performed on more than one small vessel at a pier, only one first-aid kit is required to be kept in close proximity to the work (see 29 CFR 1915.98). However, it is recommended that employers provide additional first-aid kits where needed. A facility may consult with a physician or licensed healthcare professional who is knowledgeable in occupational medicine, regarding specific first-aid needs. One person qualified to render first aid may serve several vessels as long as he/she is conveniently located near the vessels. Emergency contact numbers should be posted where the first-aid kit is maintained. On vessels in which ten or more workers are working, at least one, but not more than two, Stokes basket stretchers, or equivalent, are required to be located at each job location. Stretchers must be permanently equipped with bridles for attaching to the hoisting gear. A blanket or other liner suitable for transferring an injured worker to and from the stretcher must also be provided (see 29 CFR 1915.98(d)).

In addition to first-aid treatment, workers might be exposed to harmful substances such as lead, asbestos and cadmium. Any workers exposed to these substances, in particular, require appropriate medical surveillance. All medical exams and procedures must be performed by or under the supervision of a licensed physician, at no cost to workers and at a reasonable time and place.

Lead – An employer must institute a medical surveillance program for all workers who are or may be exposed at or above the action level (30 µg/m³ of air,

averaged over an 8-hour period) for more than 30 days a year. In addition to a detailed work and medical history, blood sampling and analysis must be made available at least every six months. If a worker's blood lead levels are at or above 40 µg/100 g of whole blood during the last sampling period, then the frequency must be increased to every two months until two consecutive blood lead levels are below 40 µg/100 g of whole blood in accord with 29 CFR 1910.1025(j)(2)(i)(B). See 29 CFR 1910.1025(j) for additional medical surveillance requirements.

Asbestos – When dealing with asbestos, the employer must institute a medical surveillance program for all workers who, for a combined total of 30 or more days per year, are engaged in Class I, II and III work or are exposed at or above a permissible exposure limit (PEL), 29 CFR 1915.1001(m)(1)(i). However, for purposes of the 30-day threshold, the employer need not count any day in which a worker engages in Class II or Class III operations on intact material for one hour or less (taking into account the entire time spent on the removal operation, including cleanup) and, while doing so, adheres fully to the work practices specified in 29 CFR 1915.1001(g).

The employer must make medical examinations and consultations available to each worker covered under paragraph 1915.1001(m)(1)(i) on the following schedules: (1) before the worker is assigned to an area where negative pressure respirators are worn; (2) within 10 working days following the thirtieth day of exposure when the worker is assigned to an area where exposure to asbestos may be at or above the PEL for 30 or more days per year, or engages in Class I, II, or III work for a combined total of 30 or more days per year; and (3) annually thereafter (see 29 CFR 1915.1001(m)(2)(i)). No worker is to be exposed to an airborne concentration of asbestos in excess of 0.1 fiber per cubic centimeter (f/cc) of air as an eight-hour time-weighted average. See 29 CFR 1915.1001(m) for additional medical surveillance requirements. Additionally, no worker is to be exposed to an airborne concentration exceeding 1.0 f/cc in a thirty-minute sampling period. See 29 CFR 1915.1001(c).

Cadmium – Under 29 CFR 1910.1027(l), an employer must institute a medical surveillance program for all workers who are or may be exposed at or above the action level (2.5 µg/m³), unless the employer can demonstrate that the worker is not, and will not be, exposed at or above the action level 30 days or more a year (twelve consecutive months). The employer must provide an initial (preplacement) examination to all workers receiving medical surveillance within 30 days after initial job assignment.

See 29 CFR 1910.1027(l)(1)(i) and (2)(i). In addition to a detailed work and medical history, biological monitoring must include: (1) cadmium in urine (CdU); (2) cadmium in blood; and (3) beta-2-micro-globulin in urine (β2-M). See 29 CFR 1910.1027(l)(2)(ii).

Worker Medical Qualifications

All workers should be physically capable of performing their tasks in a safe manner. Workers with a history of chronic back injuries should not be assigned to tasks that require manual material handling. Additionally, the employer must identify a physician or other licensed healthcare provider to perform a medical evaluation to determine a worker's ability to use a respirator. The medical evaluation can be performed either by administering a medical questionnaire or by conducting an initial medical examination that obtains the same information as the medical questionnaire (29 CFR 1910.134(e)(2)). Any abnormalities indicated on medical questionnaires may need to be evaluated by a physician specialist.

As required by 29 CFR 1915.117(c), workers with known uncorrected impaired eyesight or hearing, or who suffer from heart disease, epilepsy, or similar ailments which may suddenly incapacitate them, are prohibited from operating a crane, winch, or other power-operated hoisting apparatus.

Sanitation

Washing facilities must be provided for all workers in accordance with 29 CFR 1915.97(b). Workers must not be allowed to consume food or beverages, or to smoke in areas where they are exposed to contaminants. Workers must be instructed to wash before consuming food or beverages and smoking (see 29 CFR 1915.97(c)). Separate toilet facilities must be provided for men and women, or the facilities must be lockable (see 29 CFR 1910.141(c)).

Shipboard Rigging

Personnel assigned to perform rigging should be trained in good rigging practices. Rigging gear must be of adequate capacity to safely handle the largest anticipated load with a safety factor of no less than 5 (see 29 CFR 1915.112 and 29 CFR 1915.113). While the use of tag lines is not required in shipbreaking, care must be taken to ensure that loads are not carried over the heads of workers and that workers do not place themselves between a suspended load and a fixed object where they could be crushed (see 29 CFR 1915.116(j) and (q)). When slings attached to eye-bolts are used, the pull must be within 20 de-grees of the axis of the bolt as required by 29 CFR 1915.116(e). Only shouldered eye-bolts should be used. Wood, canvas, or other suitable materials must be used as chafing gear or softeners to prevent damage to wire rope slings[29] where they run over the edges of materials being handled (see 29 CFR 1915.116(f)). Slings should not be covered with padding that prevents them from being inspected before each use. Kinked slings, which do not straighten out when placed under load, should immediately be removed from service. Additional information regarding sling safety can be found in OSHA Publication 3072 (1996), *Sling Safety*.[30]

Workers must never be allowed to ride the load or hook (see 29 CFR 1915.116(i)). When cranes are operated "in the blind," a signalman must be assigned who is familiar with the signal codes to be used (see 29 CFR 1915.116(l)). Only this signalman must give signals to the crane operator. Hatch covers must be completely opened or removed before moving materials or equipment through them (see 29 CFR 1915.116(n)). It is recommended that the hatch beams also be removed; if not removed, the beams must be sufficiently lashed, locked, or otherwise secured to prevent them from being displaced by accident (see 29 CFR 1915.116(n)). Hatches must not be opened or closed while workers are in the square of the hatch below (see 29 CFR 1915.116(o)). Swing and travel alarms must be sounded to warn workers of movement before loads are raised, lowered, or swung (see 29 CFR 1915.116(p)). Alarms must be capable of being heard or seen above ambient noise or light levels to appropriately warn workers of potential danger (see 29 CFR 1910.165(b)(2)).

Materials Handling

During the shipbreaking process, workers handle large sections of steel and other heavy or awkward materials, resulting in unique materials handling issues that may cause injury. To the extent feasible, manual materials handling should be avoided when weights are unknown or excessive, or because of other conditions such as uneven walking surfaces, falling hazards and irregular or sharp edges of a cut plate. Mechanical materials handling methods should be used whenever possible (e.g., cranes); however, when manual materials handling is performed, gloves should be provided to protect against cuts. Walking paths[31] should be kept free from obstructions and tripping hazards. Shoes[32] should be maintained in a dry, oil-free condition, with soles and heels evenly worn.

Workers should be trained on ergonomic hazards in the workplace and about ways to minimize the risk of injury from these hazards. Some of the training topics should include: the proper use of equipment, tools and machine controls; proper lifting techniques; awareness of work tasks that may lead to pain or injury; and procedures for reporting work-related injuries and illnesses. In addition, workers should be encouraged to warm up or stretch prior to engaging in heavy lifting.[32]

Crane Services

One of the more hazardous operations in shipbreaking is handling materials with cranes.[33] Crane operations involve a complex relationship between the machine, the operator, the material being handled, the rigging and rigging gear that secures the material to the crane hook, the workers and obstructions in the area, and the ground surface or foundation of the crane. Failure, inadequate planning, or improper operation can have disastrous consequences. In 2005 alone, crane accidents.com[34] reported 127 fatalities related to crane accidents.

Only workers who are properly trained and qualified may be assigned to operate cranes in support of shipbreaking operations. Crane operators must know and understand signals used to control the crane and must be familiar with the operation of the specific machine to which they are assigned (see 29 CFR 1915.117(b) and (c)). Riggers should also be trained to safely carry out their assigned tasks.

The swing radius of the counterweight and superstructure must be established and guarded to prevent workers from being struck. Special attention should be given when cranes are operating near buildings or other structures (see 29 CFR 1915.115(d)). Loads must not be swung over the heads of workers (see 29 CFR 1915.116(j)). Both swing and travel alarms should be used to warn workers of machine movement. When lifting "in the blind," a signalman who is visible to the operator must be placed to assist the operator in safely moving the load (see 29 CFR 1915.116(l)).

Cranes used for removing materials from the ship must be certified in accord with 29 CFR 1915.115(a). A crane of sufficient capacity to safely handle the largest expected load must be used (see 29 CFR 1915.115(c)(2)). It is particularly important in selecting cut lines to consider the weight of the total load to be handled. A qualified naval architect or marine engineer should be consulted to ensure that sections cut are within the safe lifting capacity of the machine to be used. Industry practice often involves attaching the load to the crane before the final cut frees the load to avoid shock loading of the crane. The use of an electric load-indicating device is recommended to ensure that the crane or rigging is not overloaded beyond the structural safe load rating. If any recognized over-load or shock load occurs, then the crane should be removed from service until the crane and rigging are inspected in accord with the crane manufacturer's or certified agent's instructions. The crane must be maintained in accord with the manufacturer's recommendations and must be inspected in accord with applicable standards for the type of crane used. See 29 CFR 1915.111.

Crane being used to lift cut section from vessel undergoing scrapping.

Safe working loads for cranes are based on both the structural integrity of the machine and the stability of the machine on its foundation surface. Safe loading normally requires a crane to be placed on a surface with a grade of no more than 1 degree. In addition, the manufacturer's designated safe working load must not be exceeded (29 CFR 1915.115(c)(2)). Load rating charts provide no value in determining stability once the grade limitation is exceeded, thus the operation of the crane is considered unsafe beyond that point. Additionally, surfaces should be capable of safely supporting the weight of the machine and its total load. Cribbing or pads may be necessary to level the crane or to create a sufficiently stable footing. The area to be used for crane setup should be carefully selected by a person well qualified in crane operations to ensure that adequate footing is provided. The use of an engineer qualified in soil structure and stability is recommended (e.g., civil or geotechnical engineer).

Rigging must be selected to handle the largest anticipated load. Good rigging practices are required and rigging personnel should be trained in safe rigging techniques. Chafing gear should be used to protect rigging gear[35] from abrasion caused by rough edges of cut materials. Rigging gear must be inspected[36] frequently as required by 29 CFR 1915.111. Knots are not permitted in wire rope or chains.

Crane being used to lift cut section from vessel undergoing scrapping.

Fork Trucks

If fork trucks are used to move materials, only rough terrain fork trucks are recommended. Operators must be trained and must not have any condition that could cause them to become incapacitated (e.g., uncontrolled diabetes, epilepsy or heart disease) (29 CFR 1915.117(c)). Fork trucks should be of sufficient capacity for the intended load. Loads should not extend beyond the forks in a manner that could cause the fork truck to tip over. If frontend attachments are used, other than factory installed attachments, the employer must have the truck marked to identify the attachments and the appropriate weight of the truck and attachment combination (29 CFR 1910.178(a) (2)(5)). Fork trucks should be properly maintained with consideration given to the effects of the marine environment on the truck. Gasoline or diesel fork trucks should not be placed in vessel holds due to the potential for buildup of toxic gases (e.g., exhaust fumes). Fork trucks should not be driven up to workers where they might be crushed by the truck or load. Where the operator's view could be obstructed by a load, the truck should be operated with the load trailing. In situations when loads must be carried uphill they should only be driven in a forward motion and with a designated spotter. The truck path should be twice the width of the load being carried to avoid inadvertent contact with objects. An inspection must be performed on all trucks in service before each shift and at necessary intervals during its use, in accordance with 29 CFR 1915.111(a). If any item that affects the safe operation of the truck is found to be defective, the truck should be removed from service until it is repaired. For additional information see 29 CFR 1910.178 and 29 CFR 1915.117.

Trucks

Trucks may be used to haul scrap both over the road and in the yard. Trucks used over the road should be maintained in a road-worthy condition and inspected in accordance with federal and state safety regulations. The truck should be inspected daily by the driver and any condition that affects the safe use of the truck should be corrected before it is used. Trucks used in the yard should never be backed or driven up to workers standing between the truck and a fixed object. Additionally, backup alarms should be provided on these trucks when they are used in the yard to haul scrap. A spotter should be used to assist the driver when the view to the rear is obstructed. Over-the-road drivers must have a proper Commercial Driver's License. Scrap should be loaded within the safe capacity of the truck and evenly distributed over all axles, ensuring compliance with state and federal axle weight requirements. It should be loaded so as to prevent materials from shifting in or falling from the truck. While on the road, the load should be covered to prevent loose pieces from falling out. Drivers should have no condition that could cause them to become incapacitated (e.g., uncontrolled diabetes, epilepsy, or heart disease).

For More Information About Over-the-Road Truck Requirements

Federal Motor Carrier Safety Administration: Rules and Regulations www.fmcsa.dot.gov/ rules-regulations/rules-regulations.htm.

Federal Motor Carrier Safety Administration: Registration and Licensing www.fmcsa.dot. gov/ registration-licensing/registration-licensing.htm.

Powered Industrial Trucks (Forklifts) eTool, OSHA www.osha.gov/dcsp/products/etools/pit/index.html

Training

All workers engaged in shipbreaking operations must be trained in the hazards of the work to which they are exposed (e.g., persons assigned to burn materials should be trained in burning safety; riggers in rigging safety). General hazard recognition and safety precautions should be included in worker orientations, as well as training provided on the personal protective equipment (PPE) to be used at the worksite. PPE[37] training must include use of hard hats, eye protection, footwear, hearing protection, work gloves, and other PPE as appropriate (see 29 CFR 1915.152(e)). Workers should be instructed to avoid the use of synthetic clothing that melts or burns rapidly such as nylon, rayon, or Corfam®, in areas where burning operations are conducted. A daily "tool-box safety talk" to review work progress, planned work for the day and anticipated hazards associated with that work is recommended.

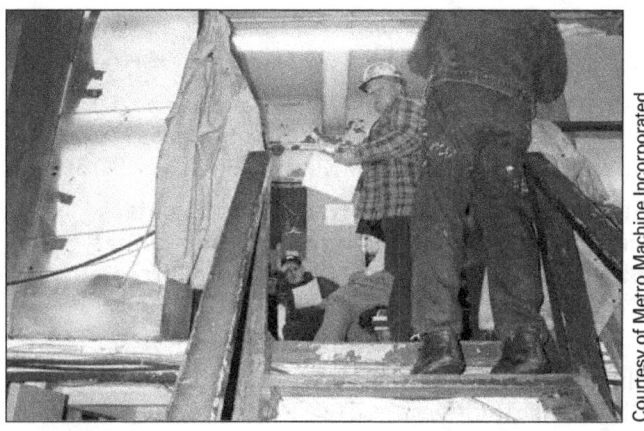

Daily safety talk.

A hazard assessment[38] of work activities, as described in 29 CFR 1915.152(b), must be conducted to determine hazards. Hazard communication[39] training must be provided to the workers and must cover the hazardous materials used in work procedures, as well as how to protect themselves from exposure to those hazards. This includes hazardous materials introduced by other employers at the worksite to which workers may be exposed. Fulfilling this requirement is the responsibility of the employer who has control over the workers performing the work. Copies of material safety data sheets (MSDSs) for hazardous materials used must be available at the worksite (29 CFR 1915.1200).

Communication

Increasingly, non-English-speaking workers are being employed in the shipbreaking industry. As a result, it has become difficult for employers and workers to communicate effectively. Despite the language barrier, signage and instructions must be understood by all workers (29 CFR 1915.16(a)). Therefore, employers may need to provide required postings and warnings in more than one language (e.g., English, Spanish, Vietnamese) at the worksite. It is important for workers to understand the hazards to which they might be exposed and the precautions necessary to avoid injury from those hazards. If workers are unable to read MSDSs or other hazard communication information themselves, then the employer should provide an interpreter to pass the information on to them.

Maintenance Shops

Maintenance shops at shipbreaking facilities have similar safety and health hazards normally encountered in other maintenance shops. As in other shops, particular attention should be paid to housekeeping, electrical safety, machine guarding and storage, and the use and disposal of hazardous materials.

References

1 http://www.epa.gov/Compliance/resources/ publications/civil/federal/shipscrap guide.pdf, A Guide for Ship Scrappers. Tips for Regulatory Compliance, EPA, Summer 2000.

2 http://www.basel.int/ships/techguid.html, Technical Guidelines for the Environmentally Sound Management of Full and Partial Dismantling of Ships, Basel Convention, August 8, 2002.

3 See note [1], above.

4 http://www.osha.gov/SLTC/etools/shipyard/ship_ breaking/index.html, eTool, Shipyard EmploymentShipbreaking, OSHA.

5 See note [4], above.

6 http://www.osha.gov/pls/oshaweb/owadisp.show_ document?p_table=STAND ARDS&p_id=10330, Regulations, Compliance Assistance Guidelines for Confined and Enclosed Spaces and Other Dangerous Atmospheres, 29 CFR 1915 Subpart B, App A, OSHA.

7 http://www.osha.gov/pls/oshaweb/owadisp.show_ document?p_table=STAND ARDS&p_id=10231, Regulations, Welding, Cutting and Heating in Way of Preservative Coating, 29 CFR 1915.53, OSHA.

8 See note [4], above.

9 http://www.osha.gov/SLTC/etools/shipyard/ standard/health_hazards.html, eTool, Shipyard Employment-General Requirements-Inventory of Hazardous Materials, OSHA.

10 http://msds.dupont.com/msds/pdfs/EN/PEN_ 09004a2f80007210.pdf, Material Safety Data Sheet for "Freon" 22, Dupont, revised April 28, 2004.

11 http://www.ask.com/bar?q=MSDS+Halon&page= 1&qsrc=2417&ab=0&u=http%3A%2F%2Fwww. wfrfire.com%2Fmsds%2Fhalon.htm, MSDS for Halon 1211, WFR Wholesale Fire and Rescue Ltd., September 2006.

12 http://www.vngas.com/pdf/g8.pdf, MSDS, BOC Gases, reviewed June 7, 1996.

13 http://www.marsulex.com/customers/pdfs/msds_ HydrogenSulfide.pdf, MSDS for Hydrogen Sulfide, Marsulex, validation date November 13, 2004.

14 http://www.osha.gov/SLTC/healthguidelines/ carbonmonoxide, Carbon Monoxide, NIOSH/OSHA Health Guidelines.

15 http://www.atsdr.cdc.gov/substances/toxsubstance. asp?toxid=22, Lead Toxic Substances Portal, Agency for Toxic Substances and Disease Registry (ATSDR) or http://www.osha.gov/pls/ oshaweb/owadisp.show_document?p_table= STANDARDS&p_id=10030, Toxic and Hazardous Substances, 29 CFR 1910.1025, OSHA.

16 http://www.osha.gov/dts/chemicalsampling/data/ CH_270900.html, Chemical Sampling Information for Tetraethyl Lead (as Pb), January 15, 1999, OSHA.

17 https://www.osha.gov/SLTC/mercury/index.html, Safety and Health Topics for Mercury, OSHA.

18 http://www.cdc.gov/niosh/ipcsneng/neng1282. html, International Chemical Safety Cards, Tributyltin Oxide, validated March 26, 1998, NIOSH.

19 http://www.osha.gov/SLTC/healthguidelines/ zincchromate/recognition.html, Occupational Safety and Health Guideline for Zinc Chromate, OSHA.

20 https://www.osha.gov/SLTC/etools/shipyard/ shiprepair/confinedspace/oxygendeficient.html, Shipyard Employment eTool, Confined or Enclosed Spaces, Oxygen-Deficient or -Enriched Atmospheres, OSHA.

21 http://www.osha.gov/OshDoc/data_MaritimeFacts/ shipbreaking-factsheet.pdf, OSHA Fact SheetShipbreaking, OSHA, 2001.

22 http://www.osha.gov/SLTC/etools/shipyard/ship_ breaking/ppe/general_ppe/life saving_equipment. html, eTool, Shipyard Employment-PPE SelectionShipbreaking-Lifesaving Equipment, OSHA.

23 http://www.osha.gov/SLTC/etools/shipyard/ship_ breaking/working_conditions/illumination.html, eTool, Shipyard Employment-Shipbreaking-Working Conditions-Illumination, OSHA.

24 http://www.osha.gov/SLTC/etools/shipyard/ship_ breaking/access/drydock_marinerailways.html, eTool, Shipyard Employment-Shipbreaking-Access-Access to and Guarding of Dry Docks and Marine Railways, OSHA.

25 See note [22], above.

26 See note [22], above.

27 http://www.epa.gov/oswer/cleanup, Cleaning Up Our Land, Water, and Air, EPA, last updated July 13, 2009.

28 http://www.osha.gov/SLTC/etools/shipyard/ship_
breaking/working_conditions/ housekeeping.html,
eTool, Shipyard Employment-Shipbreaking-Working Conditions-Housekeeping, OSHA.

29 http://www.osha.gov/Publications/osha3072.pdf,
Sling Safety, OSHA, 1996.

30 See note 28, above.

31 http://www.osha.gov/SLTC/etools/shipyard/ship_
breaking/ppe/general_ppe/foot_protection.html,
eTool, Shipyard Employment-Shipbreaking-PPE
Selection-Foot Protection, OSHA.

32 http://www.osha.gov/dsg/guidance/shipyard
guidelines.html, Guidelines for Shipyards,
Ergonomics for the Prevention of Musculoskeletal
Disorders.

33 http://www.osha.gov/SLTC/etools/shipyard/ship_
breaking/material_handling/gear.html, eTool,
Shipyard Employment-Shipbreaking-Material
Handling-Use of Gear, OSHA.

34 http://craneaccidents.com/stats.htm, Crane Accident Statistics, CraneAccidents.com.

35 http://www.osha.gov/SLTC/etools/shipyard/ship_
breaking/material_handling/ropes.html, eTool,
Shipyard Employment-Shipbreaking-Material
Handling-Ropes, Chains, and Slings, OSHA.

36 http://www.osha.gov/SLTC/etools/shipyard/ship_
breaking/material_handling/inspection.html,
eTool, Shipyard Employment-Shipbreaking-
Material handling-Inspection, OSHA.

37 http://www.osha.gov/SLTC/etools/shipyard/
standard/ppe/ppe_selection.html, eTool, Shipyard Employment-PPE-PPE Selection, OSHA.

38 http://www.osha.gov/SLTC/etools/shipyard/
standard/ppe/hazard_assessment.html, eTool,
Shipyard Employment-Hazard Assessment,
OSHA.

39 http://www.osha.gov/pls/oshaweb/owadisp.show_
document?p_table=STANDARDS&p_id=10099,
Regulations, Hazard Communication, 1910.1200,
OSHA.

Additional Resources

http://www.imo.org/includes/blastDataOnly.asp/data
_id%3D11404/ResShiprecycling962.pdf, International
Maritime Organization (IMO) Guidelines on Ship
Recycling, IMO, March 4, 2004.

http://www.ilo.org/public/english/protection/safework/
sectors/ships/shpbreak.htm, Safe Work, Ship breaking, last updated April 2000, International Labor
Office (ILO).

https://www.osha.gov/Publications/OSHA3348-
metal-scrap-recycling.pdf, Guidance for the Identifi-
cation and Control of Safety and Health Hazards in
Metal Scrap Recycling, OSHA, 2008.

http://www.osha.gov/pls/oshaweb/owadisp.show_
document?p_table=DIRECTIVES&p_ id=3224,
OSHA's National Emphasis Program (NEP) on Shipbreaking, OSHA, 3/16/05.

http://www.osha.gov/dts/maritime/index.html, OSHA
Assistance for the Maritime Industry, OSHA.

https://voa.marad.dot.gov/programs/ship_disposal/
standing_quot/docs/TECHNICAL%20COMPLIANCE
%20PLAN%20(TCP).pdf, Requirements for Technical
Compliance Plan, Maritime Administration
(MARAD).

http://www.marad.dot.gov/Offices/index.html,
MARAD Home Page.

http://www.osha.gov/dcsp/osp/index.html, State
Occupational Safety and Health Plans, OSHA.

http://www.osha.gov/pls/oshaweb/owadisp.show_
document?p_table=DIRECTIVES&p_ id=3429, Directive, CPL-02-00-142, Shipyard Employment "Tool
Bag" Directive, effective date August 3, 2006, OSHA.

www.osha.gov, OSHA Home Page.

OSHA Assistance

OSHA can provide extensive help through a variety of programs, including technical assistance about effective safety and health programs, state plans, workplace consultations, and training and education.

Safety and Health Management System Guidelines

Effective management of worker safety and health protection is a decisive factor in reducing the extent and severity of work-related injuries and illnesses and their related costs. In fact, an effective safety and health management system forms the basis of good worker protection, can save time and money, increase productivity and reduce employee injuries, illnesses and related workers' compensation costs.

To assist employers and workers in developing effective safety and health management systems, OSHA published recommended Safety and Health Program Management Guidelines (54 *Federal Register* (16): 3904-3916, January 26, 1989). These voluntary guidelines can be applied to all places of employment covered by OSHA.

The guidelines identify four general elements critical to the development of a successful safety and health management system:

- Management leadership and worker involvement,
- Worksite analysis,
- Hazard prevention and control, and
- Safety and health training.

The guidelines recommend specific actions, under each of these general elements, to achieve an effective safety and health management system. The *Federal Register* notice is available online at www.osha.gov.

State Programs

The *Occupational Safety and Health Act of 1970* (OSH Act) encourages states to develop and operate their own job safety and health plans. OSHA approves and monitors these plans. Twenty-five states, Puerto Rico and the Virgin Islands currently operate approved state plans: 22 cover both private and public (state and local government) employment; Connecticut, Illinois, New Jersey, New York and the Virgin Islands cover the public sector only. States and territories with their own OSHA-approved occupational safety and health plans must adopt standards identical to, or at least as effective as, the Federal OSHA standards.

Consultation Services

Consultation assistance is available on request to employers who want help in establishing and maintaining a safe and healthful workplace. Largely funded by OSHA, the service is provided at no cost to the employer. Primarily developed for smaller employers with more hazardous operations, the consultation service is delivered by state governments employing professional safety and health consultants. Comprehensive assistance includes an appraisal of all mechanical systems, work practices, and occupational safety and health hazards of the workplace and all aspects of the employer's present job safety and health program. In addition, the service offers assistance to employers in developing and implementing an effective safety and health program. No penalties are proposed or citations issued for hazards identified by the consultant. OSHA provides consultation assistance to the employer with the assurance that his or her name and firm and any information about the workplace will not be routinely reported to OSHA enforcement staff. For more information concerning consultation assistance, see OSHA's website at www.osha.gov.

Strategic Partnership Program

OSHA's Strategic Partnership Program helps encourage, assist and recognize the efforts of partners to eliminate serious workplace hazards and achieve a high level of worker safety and health. Most strategic partnerships seek to have a broad impact by building cooperative relationships with groups of employers and workers. These partnerships are voluntary relationships between OSHA, employers, worker representatives, and others (e.g., trade unions, trade and professional associations, universities, and other government agencies).

For more information on this and other agency programs, contact your nearest OSHA office, or visit OSHA's website at www.osha.gov.

OSHA Training and Education

OSHA area offices offer a variety of information services, such as technical advice, publications, audiovisual aids and speakers for special engagements. OSHA's Training Institute in Arlington Heights, IL, provides basic and advanced courses in safety and health for Federal and state compliance officers, state consultants, Federal agency personnel, and private sector employers, workers and their representatives.

The OSHA Training Institute also has established OSHA Training Institute Education Centers to address the increased demand for its courses from the private sector and from other federal agencies. These centers are colleges, universities, and nonprofit organizations that have been selected after a competition for participation in the program.

OSHA also provides funds to nonprofit organizations, through grants, to conduct workplace training and education in subjects where OSHA believes there is a lack of workplace training. Grants are awarded annually.

For more information on grants, training and education, contact the OSHA Training Institute, Directorate of Training and Education, 2020 South Arlington Heights Road, Arlington Heights, IL 60005, (847) 297-4810, or see Training on OSHA's website at www.osha.gov. For further information on any OSHA program, contact your nearest OSHA regional office listed at the end of this publication.

Information Available Electronically

OSHA has a variety of materials and tools available on its website at www.osha.gov. These include electronic tools, such as *Safety and Health Topics, eTools, Expert Advisors*; regulations, directives and publications; videos and other information for employers and workers. OSHA's software programs and eTools walk you through challenging safety and health issues and common problems to find the best solutions for your workplace.

OSHA Publications

OSHA has an extensive publications program. For a listing of free items, visit OSHA's website at www.osha.gov or contact the OSHA Publications Office, U.S. Department of Labor, 200 Constitution Avenue, NW, N-3101, Washington, DC 20210; telephone (202) 693-1888 or fax to (202) 693-2498.

Contacting OSHA

To report an emergency, file a complaint, or seek OSHA advice, assistance, or products, call (800) 321-OSHA or contact your nearest OSHA Regional or Area office listed at the end of this publication. The teletypewriter (TTY) number is (877) 889-5627.

Written correspondence can be mailed to the nearest OSHA Regional or Area Office listed at the end of this publication or to OSHA's national office at: U.S. Department of Labor, Occupational Safety and Health Administration, 200 Constitution Avenue, N.W., Washington, DC 20210.

By visiting OSHA's website at www.osha.gov, you can also:

- File a complaint online,
- Submit general inquiries about workplace safety and health electronically, and
- Find more information about OSHA and occupational safety and health.

OSHA Regional Offices

Region I
(CT*, ME, MA, NH, RI, VT*)
JFK Federal Building, Room E340
Boston, MA 02203
(617) 565-9860

Region II
(NJ*, NY*, PR*, VI*)
201 Varick Street, Room 670
New York, NY 10014
(212) 337-2378

Region III
(DE, DC, MD*, PA, VA*, WV)
The Curtis Center
170 S. Independence Mall West
Suite 740 West
Philadelphia, PA 19106-3309
(215) 861-4900

Region IV
(AL, FL, GA, KY*, MS, NC*, SC*, TN*)
61 Forsyth Street, SW, Room 6T50
Atlanta, GA 30303
(404) 562-2300

Region V
(IL*, IN*, MI*, MN*, OH, WI)
230 South Dearborn Street
Room 3244
Chicago, IL 60604
(312) 353-2220

Region VI
(AR, LA, NM*, OK, TX)
525 Griffin Street, Room 602
Dallas, TX 75202
(972) 850-4145

Region VII
(IA*, KS, MO, NE)
Two Pershing Square
2300 Main Street, Suite 1010
Kansas City, MO 64108-2416
(816) 283-8745

Region VIII
(CO, MT, ND, SD, UT*, WY*)
1999 Broadway, Suite 1690
PO Box 46550
Denver, CO 80202-5716
(720) 264-6550

Region IX
(AZ*, CA*, HI*, NV*, and American Samoa,
Guam and the Northern Mariana Islands)
90 7th Street, Suite 18-100
San Francisco, CA 94103
(415) 625-2547

Region X
(AK*, ID, OR*, WA*)
1111 Third Avenue, Suite 715
Seattle, WA 98101-3212
(206) 553-5930

* These states and territories operate their own OSHA-approved job safety and health programs and cover state and local government employees as well as private sector employees. The Connecticut, Illinois, New Jersey, New York and Virgin Islands plans cover public employees only. States with approved programs must have standards that are identical to, or at least as effective as, the Federal OSHA standards.

Note: To get contact information for OSHA Area Offices, OSHA-approved State Plans and OSHA Consultation Projects, please visit us online at www.osha.gov or call us at 1-800-321-OSHA.